Yoga for Kids

Simple Animal Poses for Any Age

Library of Congress Cataloging-in-Publication data is on file with the publisher.

© 2013 Edizioni Corsare
© 2015 for this book in the English language—Albert Whitman & Company
Text by Lorena V. Pajalunga
Pictures by Anna Forlati
Original title: Yoga piccolo piccolo
Published by arrangement with Atlantyca S.p.A.
ISBN 978-0-8075-9172-7

For information, address Atlantyca S.p.A, Via Leopardi 8, 20123 Milano, Italia.
foreignrights@atlantyca.it
www.atlantyca.com

Printed in China
10 9 8 7 6 5 4 3 2 1 HH 20 19 18 17 16 15

For more information about Albert Whitman & Company,
visit our web site at www.albertwhitman.com.

Yoga for Kids

Simple Animal Poses for Any Age

Lorena V. Pajalunga

pictures by Anna Forlati

Albert Whitman & Company
Chicago, Illinois

Mom signed me up for yoga lessons at the zoo.

The instructor told our class that *yoga* means "union of the mind and the heart" and that this ancient philosophy comes from India.

The instructor said the word *philosophy* means "love of knowledge."

During our lessons I learned new games, how to breathe better, and how to relax, and we tried some meditation exercises.

What I enjoyed most were the *asanas*, the many different body positions that you must try to hold.

I thought it would be strange to practice yoga at the zoo...

But that was
before I realized so
many yoga poses resemble
the animals there!

After my lessons, I go home where my cat, Nino, waits for me. He's a master of relaxation, so I practice my yoga with him and teach him the poses I learned at the zoo. First is the king of the beasts: the **LION**!

I sit on my heels, with my hands on the ground and my fingers pointing toward me.

I close my eyes and take a deep breath. I open my mouth wide and roar loudly! Then I stick out my tongue.

The next pose I show Nino is
the old **TORTOISE**. I sit down with
my feet parallel and knees bent.
My hands slide under my legs to hold
my feet. I breathe out and then try to
touch my feet with my forehead.
When I look at Nino, he's
happily snoozing.

I shiver when I think of the **KING COBRA** rising up to strike its prey.

To do this pose, I lie on my stomach with my legs together and stretched straight out behind me. I place my hands below my shoulders. I raise my head, my shoulders, and my back, straightening my arms completely. I can feel my heart filling with courage. I try to hiss.

Then I try to touch my head with my feet. But this is very hard!

I show Nino what it looks like to be a **SEAGULL**. Standing, I lean forward a little and open my arms like a bird that's gliding through the air to land on a rock.

Next is a very special position. I kneel, rest my feet on the floor, and grasp my ankles. Our instructor said I can grasp my heels if I can't reach. Then I push my hips as far forward as I can and allow my head to fall back.

Do I look like a **CAMEL**?

There were no dogs at the zoo but we did see wolves. My instructor showed us the stretching **DOG** position. Come on, Nino. Let's try it.

I make an upside-down V shape with my body. My hands are in front of me, aligned with my head, neck, and back. My legs are together and my heels are on the floor. I push my hips up.

What are you doing, Nino? He must not want to look like a dog!

The **TIGER** looks like you, Nino—but I bet he's not as lazy!

I get onto all fours. Then I breathe out as I bring my knee up to my forehead, curving my back. Then, without putting my leg back down, I hold it out behind me.

Then I turn my head and growl. GRRRRRRR!

Now I repeat it with my other leg on the other side.

Nino just purrs.

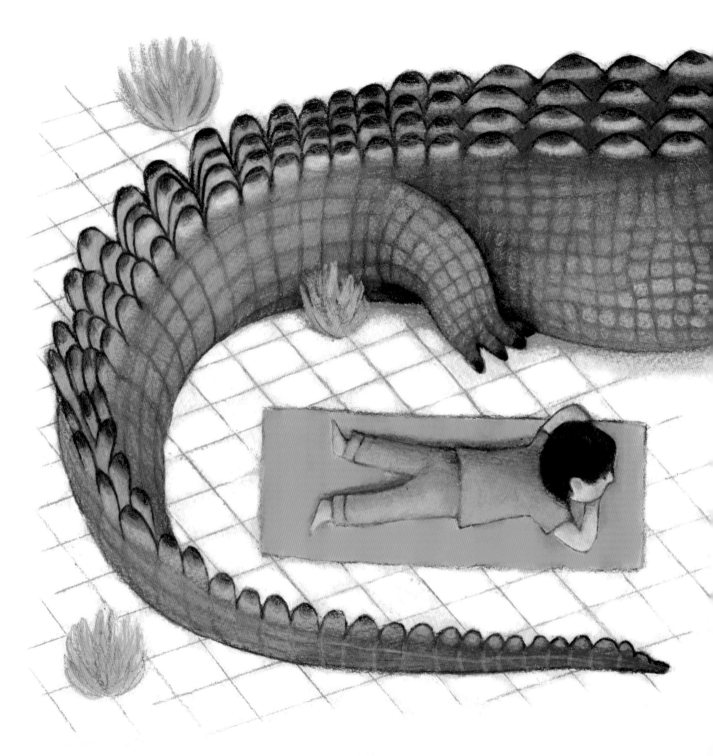

Next I have a little rest, just like a **CROCODILE**.
Lying on my stomach, I place my hands on top
of each other and rest my head on them. My feet
are slightly apart and my heels face inward.

This feels good! Now I know why Nino spends
so much time relaxing.

Did you know that an **EAGLE** can have a wingspan of ten feet, Nino?

Standing on my left foot, I wrap my right leg around my left one, trying to hook my right foot behind my left knee.

My arms form the eagle's beak. My left arm is in front of me, slightly bent. My right arm goes under the left one and my hands touch.

I read that a **FLAMINGO** can stand on one leg for a very long time.

I open my arms, bend forward, and try to balance on just one leg. How long can I stay like this? How long will Nino sleep?

My yoga instructor taught me a little secret: if I stare at a point in front of me, I can keep my balance much longer.

Nino, look! There is a position named after you too. Watch me do the **CAT** pose!

On all fours, I round and then arch my back, just like you!

But you do it better.

My yoga lessons taught me so much and
we got to meet so many animals. We saw
the brave **LION**,
the slow **TORTOISE**,
the strong **COBRA**,
the soaring **SEAGULL**,
the funny **CAMEL**,
the friendly **DOG**,
the noble **TIGER**,
the great **CROCODILE**,
the elegant **EAGLE**,
the graceful **FLAMINGO**,
and my friend, Nino, the knowing **CAT**!

TIPS FOR PRACTICING YOGA

❈ Wear comfortable clothes that stretch when you move. For stability and comfort, remove your socks and shoes.

❈ Listen to your body—if it doesn't feel good, don't do it. It takes practice to master certain moves, so be patient. You might not get it right the first time.

❈ A yoga mat is a good way to ensure you have a comfortable and slip-free surface on which to practice. But a mat is not necessary to practice yoga, so don't worry if you don't have one.

❈ Practice yoga somewhere quiet where you can rest your mind. Try to turn off televisions and computers or any other distracting sounds. Playing quiet, soothing music is fine.

❈ Above all, relax! For the most positive yoga experience, clear your mind and loosen your body.